Published by Abinash Sathiharu Publishing

FLIGHT ATTENDANT
NUTRITION FACTS

AMOUNT PER SERVING: **1 GREAT FLIGHT ATTENDANT**

% DAILY VALUE**

HARD WORK	1000%
SLEEP	0%
TALENT	500%
PASSION	100%
DEDICATION	300%
CAFFEINE	110%

*Percentage daily values are based on your unique diet

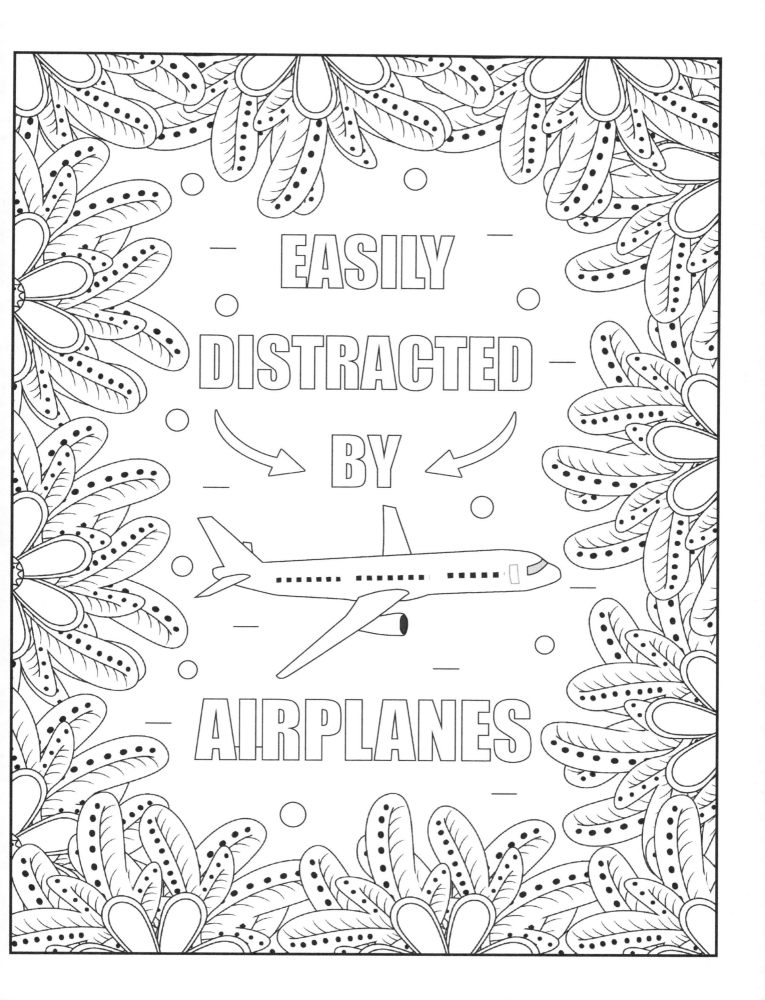

Made in United States
Orlando, FL
12 July 2023